A Note From Rick Renner

I am on a personal quest to see a "revival of the Bible" so people can establish their lives on a firm foundation that will stand strong and endure the test when the end-time storm winds begin to intensify.

In order to experience a revival of the Bible in your personal life, it is important to take time each day to read, receive, and apply its truths to your life. James tells us that if we will continue in the perfect law of liberty — refusing to be forgetful hearers but determined to be doers — we will be blessed in our ways. As you watch or listen to the programs in this series and work through this corresponding study guide, I trust that you will search the Scriptures and allow the Holy Spirit to help you hear something new from God's Word that applies specifically to your life. I encourage you to be a doer of the Word that He reveals to you. Whatever the cost, I assure you — it will be worth it.

> Thy words were found, and I did eat them;
> and thy word was unto me the joy and rejoicing of mine heart:
> for I am called by thy name, O Lord God of hosts.
> — Jeremiah 15:16

Your brother and friend in Jesus Christ,

Rick Renner

Running Your Race With Purpose

Copyright © 2020 by Rick Renner
8316 E. 73rd St.
Tulsa, Oklahoma 74133

Published by Rick Renner Ministries
www.renner.org

ISBN 13: 978-1-68031-802-9

eBook ISBN 13: 978-1-68031-803-6

How To Use This Study Guide

This five-lesson study guide corresponds to *"Running Your Race With Purpose" With Rick Renner* (Renner TV). Each lesson in this study guide covers a topic that is addressed during the program series, with questions and references supplied to draw you deeper into your own private study of the Scriptures on this subject.

To derive the most benefit from this study guide, consider the following:

First, watch or listen to the program prior to working through the corresponding lesson in this guide. (Programs can also be viewed at **renner.org** by clicking on the Media/Archives links.)

Second, take the time to look up the scriptures included in each lesson. Prayerfully consider their application to your own life.

Third, use a journal or notebook to make note of your answers to each lesson's Study Questions and Practical Application challenges.

Fourth, invest specific time in prayer and in the Word of God to consult with the Holy Spirit. Write down the scriptures or insights He reveals to you.

Finally, take action! Whatever the Lord tells you to do according to His Word, do it.

For added insights on this subject, it is recommended that you obtain Rick Renner's book *A Life Ablaze: Ten Simple Keys To Living on Fire for God.* You may also select from Rick's other available resources by placing your order at **renner.org** or by calling 1-800-742-5593.

TOPIC

What Race Are You Called To Run?

SCRIPTURES

1. **1 Corinthians 9:24** — Know ye not that they which run in a race run all, but one receiveth the prize? So run that ye may obtain.

2. **Ephesians 1:4** — According as he hath chosen us in him before the foundation of the world...

3. **Ephesians 2:10** — For we are his workmanship, created in Christ Jesus unto good works, which God hath before ordained that we should walk in them.

GREEK WORDS

1. "know" — οἶδα (*oida*): to see, perceive, understand, or comprehend

2. "not" — οὐκ (*ouk*): an emphatic form of "no"; emphatically, categorically not

3. "run" — τρέχω (*trecho*): to run, but the form here pictures one who is running; pictures one who has jumped into the race and is pressing ahead with all his might to reach a goal set before him; one who is running at such a pace that both feet never hit the ground at the same time; with eyes fixed on the finish line, the runner makes a run for it, steadily moving forward toward the goal

4. "race" — στάδιον (*stadion*): a race course that was 600 feet in length or one eighth of a Roman mile; the exact length used in the Olympics of the ancient world and in the Isthmian Games held near the city of Corinth; it eventually became the word for a stadium, a place where athletic competitions were held; those participating in these games were noted for being disciplined, balanced, and committed to excellence

5. "run" — τρέχω (*trecho*): to run, but the form here pictures one who is running; pictures one who has jumped into the race and is pressing ahead with all his might to reach a goal set before him; one who is running at such a pace that both feet never hit the ground at the same

time; with eyes fixed on the finish line, the runner makes a run for it, steadily moving forward toward the goal

6. "all" — πάντες (*pantes*): all, indicating every single person in each race

7. "one" — εἷς (*heis*): one; refers to one and one only

8. "receiveth" — λαμβάνω (*lambano*): to seize or to lay hold of something in order to make it your very own, almost like a person who reaches out to grab, capture, or take possession of something; in some cases, it means to violently lay hold of something in order to seize and take it as one's very own; at other times, it depicts one who graciously receives something that is freely and easily given

9. "prize" — βραβεῖον (*brabeion*): describes the prizes and rewards given to victors who won in the games; the prize that follows a triumph; also depicts the umpire, referee, or judge who moderated and judged athletic competitions

10. "chosen" — ἐκλέγομαι (*eklegomai*): a compound of ἐκ (*ek*) and λέγω (*lego*); the word ἐκ (*ek*) means out and the word λέγω (*lego*) means "I say"; compounded, "Out, I say"; to choose, elect, or select; to pick out or choose for oneself; portrays a deliberate choice

11. "before" — πρό (*pro*): before; in front of; before in terms of time

12. "foundation" — καταβολή (*katabole*): a compound of κατά (*kata*) and βάλλω (*ballo*); the word κατά (*kata*) means down and βάλλω (*ballo*) means to throw or to hurl; the first hurling of the universe into place; a reference to the first acts of creation

13. "world" — κόσμος (*kosmos*): the world, universe, or anything ordered; creation

14. "workmanship" — ποίημα (*poiema*): a masterful work carried out at the hands of a Master

15. "created" — κτίζω (*ktidzo*): create, form, shape; even carries the idea of design

16. "unto" — ἐπί (*epi*): for; specially for; indicates express purpose

17. "before ordained" — προετοιμάζω (*proetoimadzo*): a compound of πρό (*pro*) and ἐτοιμάζω (*hetoimadzo*); the word πρό (*pro*) means before, in front of, or before in terms of time; the word ἐτοιμάζω (*hetoimadzo*) means to make ready, prepare: to make the necessary preparations, get everything ready, full readiness and preparation; compounded, it means to previously do everything necessary to make ready and fully prepared

18. "walk" — περιπατέω (*peripateo*): to walk around, to live and carry on in one general vicinity; pictures a person who has walked on one path or vicinity for so long that he can now almost walk that path blindfolded; suggests one who has walked in one region for so long that it has now become his environment, his place of daily activity; often translated to live; to stroll

SYNOPSIS

The five lessons in this study on *Running Your Race With Purpose* will focus on the following topics:

- What Race Are You Called To Run?
- What Reward Do You Want To Obtain?
- Temporary and Eternal Rewards
- What Is Your Strategy To Reach Your Goal?
- What Is a Castaway?

The emphasis of this lesson:

Spiritually speaking, you are in a race, and God wants you to run your race in order to win the prize. He personally selected you before the foundation of the world to be on His team. You are not an accident or a mistake.

Located just a few short miles from the city of Corinth was the town of Isthmia. Although it was small in size, every two years it hosted a series of athletic games, very similar to the Olympics. During that time, Isthmia would swell with both visitors and contestants from everywhere. Because of its close proximity to Corinth, many Corinthians would make the journey to watch the games.

Of all the contests, the footraces were the most popular. This is why the apostle Paul used illustrations of a footrace when he wrote to the Corinthian believers. This helps us understand the context for what he said in First Corinthians 9:24: "Know ye not that they which run in a race run all, but one receiveth the prize? So run that ye may obtain."

Realize That You Are in a Race

There are several important words to understand in First Corinthians 9:24. For instance, the word "know" is the Greek word *oida*, which means *to see, perceive, understand, or comprehend.* The word "not" is the Greek word *ouk*, which is an emphatic form of the word "no." It means *emphatically, categorically not.* Thus, when Paul said, "Know ye not," it is the equivalent of him saying, "Have you guys not gotten it yet? Has it not gotten through to you? How do you possibly not understand?"

What didn't these early believers fully grasp? It was the fact that as runners in a spiritual race, they were called to "run." This word "run" is a form of the Greek word *trecho*, which means *to run*, but the form here pictures *one who is running.* It depicts *one who has jumped into the race and is pressing ahead with all his might to reach a goal set before him; one who is running at such a pace that both feet never hit the ground at the same time.* With his eyes fixed on the finish line, this runner makes a run for it, steadily moving forward toward the goal.

All the Corinthian believers understood what Paul was trying to communicate because they had attended the nearby Isthmian games and watched how the runners removed all distractions from their field of vision as they pressed toward the finish line. They were in the race to win it.

The word "race" in this verse is the Greek word *stadion*, and it describes *a race course that was 600 feet in length or one eighth of a Roman mile.* This was the exact length used in the Olympics of the ancient world and in the Isthmian Games held near the city of Corinth. The word *stadion* eventually became the word for a *stadium*, a place where athletic competitions were held. Those participating in these games were noted for being disciplined, balanced, and committed to excellence.

By using the word *stadion*, Paul was telling the Corinthians — and us — that if we're going to reach our goal and take hold of our prize, we have to be committed, balanced, and determined to be our very best. Again, we are to "run" — from the Greek word *trecho* — which means *to totally focus on the goal line and remove all distractions.*

We Are To Run To Win the Prize

It is important to note that the Scripture says "all" run. The word "all" in Greek is *pantes*, which means *all*, indicating *every single person in each race.*

Paul went on to say, "...But one receiveth the prize" (1 Corinthians 9:24). In Greek, the word "one" is *heis*, meaning *one*; it refers to *one and one only*. In the ancient games, only one person received the prize.

The word "receiveth" is a form of the Greek word *lambano*, which means *to seize or to lay hold of something in order to make it your very own* — almost like a person who reaches out to grab, capture, or take possession of something. In some cases, it means *to violently lay hold of something in order to seize and take it as one's very own*. At other times, it depicts *one who graciously receives something that is freely and easily given*. This is how it is in our relationship with God. He graciously gives us His grace and everything we need to live a godly life, but we must reach out and seize it by faith.

Paul said we are to run in such a way to receive the "prize." The word "prize" is the Greek word *brabeion*, which describes *the prizes and rewards given to victors who won in the games; the prize that follows a triumph*. This word also depicts *the umpire, referee, or judge who moderated and judged athletic competitions and waited at the finish line for the first person to cross*. That one winner was awarded the prize. No trophies or ribbons were given to the other participants.

Friend, you are no accident. God brought you into this world for a specific purpose. He didn't give you life just to take up space and then one day go to Heaven. He has a specific assignment exclusively for you to carry out, and He has gifted you to accomplish it. The question is, do you know what race God has asked you to run? What is your calling — what are you supposed to achieve with your life?

You Were Handpicked By God

Speaking through the apostle Paul, the Holy Spirit makes it quite clear that your life has great meaning. The Bible says, "According as he hath chosen us in him before the foundation of the world..." (Ephesians 1:4). Notice the word "chosen." It is the Greek word *eklegomai*, a compound of the words *ek* and *lego*. The word *ek* means *out*, and the word *lego* means *"I say."* When these two words are compounded to form *eklegomai*, it literally means *"Out, I say."* It can also mean *to choose, elect, or select; to pick out or choose for oneself*, indicating *a deliberate choice*.

The use of this word is a picture of God looking into the future and seeing us and saying, "Hey, I'm calling you out. I'm purposefully selecting you for Myself." When did God make the decision to choose you? The Bible says, "…He hath chosen us in him before the foundation of the world…" Ephesians 1:4).

In Greek, the word "before" is the word *pro*, which means *before* or *in front of; before in terms of time*. The word "foundation" is the Greek word *katabole*, which is a compound of the word *kata*, meaning *down*, and *ballo*, meaning *to throw or to hurl*. It indicates *the first hurling of the universe into place*; it is *a reference to the first acts of creation*. This brings us to the word "world," which is the Greek word *kosmos* and describes *the world, universe, or anything ordered; creation*. Before anything ever came into existence — before the formation of the sun, moon, and stars and before the creation of the vegetation and animal life — God chose you to be His own.

Taking into account the original Greek meaning, here is the *Renner Interpretive Version (RIV)* of Ephesians 1:4:

> **Even before the first layer of the earth's foundation was laid, God was already peering into the future and He saw us there! When He saw us, He spoke, and said, "Out!" When he said those words, he literally "selected" us as His own.**

You Are God's 'Workmanship'

Just a few verses later, in Ephesians 2:10, the apostle Paul made this remarkable declaration: "For we are his workmanship, created in Christ Jesus unto good works, which God hath before ordained that we should walk in them."

The word "workmanship" is a form of the Greek word *poiema*, and it describes *a masterful work carried out at the hands of a Master*. It is from where we get the word *poem*. The word "created" is the Greek word *ktidzo*, which means *to create, form, or shape*. It carries the idea of *a creative work with a special design*. We are God's workmanship created "unto good works." Even the word "unto" is significant. It is the Greek word *epi*, and it means *specially for*, indicating *express purpose*.

The Bible says the good works we were created for were "before ordained" — the Greek word *proetoimadzo*. It is a compound of the word *pro*, meaning *before, in front of, or before in terms of time*; and the word *hetoimadzo*, meaning *to make ready, prepare*: *to make the necessary preparations, get everything ready, full readiness and preparation*. When these two words are compounded to form *proetoimadzo*, it means *to previously do everything necessary to make ready and fully prepared.*

From before the foundation of the earth, it has been God's desire that we "walk" in the good works He preplanned. The word "walk" is the Greek word *peripateo*, which means *to walk around, to live and carry on in one general vicinity.* It pictures *a person who has walked on one path or vicinity for so long that he can now almost walk that path blindfolded.* This word suggests *one who has walked in one region for so long that it has now become his environment, his place of daily activity.* The word *peripateo* is often translated *to live* or *to stroll,* which indicates that God wants us to be so aware of what He has called us to do that it becomes our comfortable abode.

Again, you are God's "workmanship" — from the Greek word *poiema,* which carries the idea of *something artfully created.* Interestingly, the Greek word for a poet, *poites,* comes from this same word. In regards to a poet, this word depicts *one who has extraordinary ability to write or create a literary masterpiece.*

The fact that Paul used this word *poiema* to explain what took place when you became a child of God emphatically means that the day you got saved, God exerted His most powerful and creative effort to make you new. And once He was finished creating you new, you became *a masterpiece, skillfully and artfully created in Christ Jesus.* This tells us that there is nothing cheap about you. *God's creative artistic, intelligent genius went into making you!*

Friend, your life is no mistake or accident. God handpicked you before the foundation of the world to be His treasured child and to do something magnificent to bring Him glory. This is the specific "race" marked out for you to run. Once you discover your God-given destiny and begin to go after it with all you've got, your life will take on a vibrant fullness that is truly life-giving.

In our next lesson, we are going to see what kinds of rewards await you as you pursue God's purpose for your life.

STUDY QUESTIONS

Study to shew thyself approved unto God, a workman that needeth not to be ashamed, rightly dividing the word of truth.
— 2 Timothy 2:15

1. Did you know that you were purposely handpicked by God to play a part in His-story? Take a look at these amazing verses, reading them as if God were saying them directly to you. What stands out to you personally?

   - Jeremiah 1:5

   - Isaiah 49:1-3

   - Psalm 139:13-16

   - John 15:16

   - Ephesians 1:6

2. What aspects of God's love and acceptance do you see now that you didn't see before?

PRACTICAL APPLICATION

**But be ye doers of the word, and not hearers only,
deceiving your own selves.
—James 1:22**

1. You are not a mistake or an accident. You've been birthed on the earth for a purpose. Do you know what that purpose is? Are you aware of the "race" God has asked *you* to run? If so, briefly describe what you understand it to be.

2. Rick shared on the program how when he was growing up, he tried playing several different types of sports, but he was never really interested in any of them. He was drawn to museums, symphonies, and magnificent works of art. When you were younger, what activities did *you* try but never seemed to excel at? What interests were you consistently drawn to and fascinated by? What do your answers say to you about your purpose?

3. Have you ever felt like you were a mistake or that your life was an accident? If so, what has caused you to think that way? How is this lesson helping you see and believe the truth — that you were created *on purpose, for a purpose?*

TOPIC

What Reward Do You Want To Obtain?

SCRIPTURES

1. **Ephesians 1:4** — According as he hath chosen us in him before the foundation of the world...

2. **Ephesians 2:10** — For we are his workmanship, created in Christ Jesus unto good works, which God hath before ordained that we should walk in them.

3. **1 Corinthians 9:24** — Know ye not that they which run in a race run all, but one receiveth the prize? So run that ye may obtain.

4. **John 15:16** — Ye have not chosen me, but I have chosen you, and ordained you, that ye should go and bring forth fruit...

GREEK WORDS

1. "chosen" — ἐκλέγομαι (*eklegomai*): a compound of ἐκ (*ek*) and λέγω (*lego*); the word ἐκ (*ek*) means out and the word λέγω (*lego*) means "I say"; compounded, "Out, I say"; to choose, elect, or select; to pick out or choose for oneself; portrays a deliberate choice

2. "ordained" — τίθημι (*tithemi*): to set in place; to fix in place; to establish

3. "fruit" — καρπός (*karpos*): the physical fruit of plants or trees; depicts the fruit borne by a person's life; this fruit might include a person's deeds, actions, moral character, and behavior, or the output of the person's work; the word describes the by-product of a plant or tree, or a person's life

4. "know" — οἶδα (*oida*): to see, perceive, understand, or comprehend

5. "not" — οὐκ (*ouk*): an emphatic form of "no"; emphatically, categorically not

6. "run" — τρέχω (*trecho*): to run, but the form here pictures one who is running; pictures one who has jumped into the race and is pressing ahead with all his might to reach a goal set before him; one who is running at such a pace that both feet never hit the ground at the same

time; with eyes fixed on the finish line, the runner makes a run for it, steadily moving forward toward the goal

7. "race" — **στάδιον** (*stadion*): a race course that was 600 feet in length or one-eighth of a Roman mile, the exact length used in the Olympics of the ancient world and in the Isthmian Games held near the city of Corinth; it eventually became the word for a stadium, a place where athletic competitions were held; those participating in these games were noted for being disciplined, balanced, and committed to excellence

8. "all" — **πάντες** (*pantes*): all, indicating every single person in each race

9. "one" — **εἷς** (*heis*): one; refers to one and one only

10. "receiveth" — **λαμβάνω** (*lambano*): to seize or to lay hold of something in order to make it your very own, almost like a person who reaches out to grab, capture, or take possession of something; in some cases, it means to violently lay hold of something in order to seize and take it as one's very own; at other times, it depicts one who graciously receives something that is freely and easily given

11. "prize" — **βραβεῖον** (*brabeion*): describes the prizes and rewards given to victors who won in the games; the prize that follows a triumph; also depicts the umpire, referee, or judge who moderated and judged athletic competitions

12. "so" — **οὕτως** (*houtos*): in this way; in this manner; in line with this; accordingly

13. "obtain" — **καταλαμβάνω** (*katalambano*): to grab hold of; to seize; to wrestle; to pull down; to master and to make your very own; pictures one pouncing, seizing or latching hold of a thing with all of his might; depicts a runner who runs with all his energy to obtain, seize, tackle, conquer, comprehend, overtake, or master the prize

SYNOPSIS

In our first lesson, we took a close look at First Corinthians 9:24 and learned that each and every believer — including you — has been called by God to run a specific race. Contrary to what you may have heard from others, your life is not an accident or a mistake. God brought you into this world for a specific purpose. He has personally selected you to carry out a special assignment, and He has gifted you to accomplish it. The question is, do you know what race God has asked you to run? And what rewards do you desire to obtain with your life?

The emphasis of this lesson:

You are God's masterpiece created in Christ Jesus to do good works. Jesus chose you and established you to produce lasting fruit. As you run the race you've been called to run, you will be empowered to grab hold of everything God has destined for your life.

You Are No Accident or Mistake — God Chose You!

Have you ever heard someone say, "My parents didn't plan me. I was an accident no one expected." A few people use this as an excuse for not accepting responsibility in life, claiming that they are just accidents who came into the world by mistake. But if you are a believer, you are not a mistake or an accident.

The apostle Paul made this clear when he wrote, "According as He hath chosen us in him before the foundation of the world..." (Ephesians 1:4). The word "chosen" in this verse is very significant. It is the Greek word *eklegomai*, a compound of the words *ek* and *lego*. The word *ek* means *out*, and the word *lego* means *I say*. Together, these words literally mean *"Out, I say!"* It can also mean *to call out, to select, to elect*, or *to personally choose*.

In classical Greek writings, the word *eklegó* referred to a person or a group of people who were *selected* for a special purpose. For instance, this word *eklegó* was used for the selection of men for military service. It was also used to denote soldiers who were *chosen out of* the entire military to go on a special mission or to do a special task. Finally, it was used for politicians who were *elected* by the general public to hold a public position or to execute a special job on behalf of the community. In every case where this word *eklegó* — translated here as "chosen" — is used to portray the election or selection of individuals, it conveys the idea of *the great privilege and honor of being chosen*.

It also speaks of the responsibility placed on those who are chosen to walk, act, and live in a way that is honorable to their calling. Because of the great privilege of being elected to a higher position or selected to perform a special task, those who are "chosen" — which includes us — bear a responsibility to walk and act in accordance with the calling that has been extended to them. They should look upon themselves as chosen, honored, esteemed, and respected — special representatives of the one who elected them!

So when Paul says that God "…had chosen us in him before the foundation of the world…," he is saying that God looked out to the horizon of human history — *and He saw us*! How amazing! And when God saw us, His voice echoed forth from Heaven: "Out, I say!" In that flash, our destinies were divinely sealed!

Taking into account the original Greek meaning, here is the *Renner Interpretive Version (RIV)* of Ephesians 1:4:

> **Even before the first layer of the earth's foundation was laid, God was already peering into the future and He saw us there! When He saw us, He spoke, and said, "Out!" When he said those words, he literally "selected" us as His own.**

You Are God's 'Masterpiece'

In Ephesians 2:10, Paul builds on this truth declaring, "For we are his workmanship, created in Christ Jesus unto good works, which God hath before ordained that we should walk in them."

We saw that the word "workmanship" is a form of the Greek word *poiema*, and it describes *a masterful work carried out at the hands of a Master*. It conveys the idea of *something artfully created*. Interestingly, the Greek word for a poet, *poietes*, comes from this same word. In regards to a poet, this Greek word depicts *one who has extraordinary ability to write or create a literary masterpiece*.

Because Paul used this word *poiema* to explain what took place when you became a child of God, it emphatically means that the day you got saved, God exerted His most powerful and creative effort to make you new. And once He was finished making you new, you became *a masterpiece, skillfully and artfully created in Christ Jesus*. This tells us that there is nothing cheap about you! *God's creative artistic, intelligent genius went into making you!*

Paul went on to say that we are "…created in Christ Jesus unto good works, which God hath before ordained that we should walk in them" (Ephesians 2:10). The word "created" is the Greek word *ktidzo*, which means *to create, form, or shape*. And the word "unto" is the Greek word *epi*, which indicates *for the express purpose*.

In this part of the verse, God is communicating through Paul and letting you know that you were created for the express purpose of doing good works. He prepared everything ahead of time so that you would "walk" in them. The word "walk" here is the Greek word *peripateo*, which means *to walk around, to live and carry on in one general vicinity*. This word depicts *one who has habitually walked in one region for so long that it has now become his environment, his place of daily activity*. This word *peripateo* is often translated *to live* or *to stroll*, which means that God wants us to be so mindful of what He has called us to do that it becomes our dwelling place.

Jesus Chose You To Bear 'Fruit'

What is interesting is that Jesus said some of the very same things about you just before He was crucified on the Cross and rose from the grave. In John 15:16, He said, "Ye have not chosen me, but I have chosen you, and ordained you, that ye should go and bring forth fruit." The word "chosen," which appears twice in this verse, is again the Greek word *eklegomai*. It is a compound of the word *ek*, meaning *out*, and the word *lego*, which means *I say*. When these words are compounded, it is the equivalent of Jesus looking at us and saying, "Hey you... Out, I say!" It means He has selected us, commissioned us, and anointed us for a special task.

In fact, not only did Jesus choose us, but He also "ordained" us. In Greek, the word "ordained" is a form of the word *tithemi*, which in this verse means *to set in place*; *to fix in place*; or *to establish*. When Jesus chose us, He also *set us in place* and *established us* to bring forth "fruit."

The word for "fruit" here is the Greek word *karpos*. Although it normally describes the physical fruit of plants or trees, in this case it depicts *the fruit borne by a person's life*. This fruit might include *a person's deeds, actions, moral character, and behavior*, or *the total output of the person's work*. Therefore, the word *karpos* describes *the by-product of a plant or tree, or a person's life*.

You Have a Race To Run

Turning our attention once again to First Corinthians 9:24, it says, "Know ye not that they which run in a race run all, but one receiveth the prize? So run that ye may obtain."

We saw that the word "know" is the Greek word *oida*, which means *to see, perceive, understand, or comprehend*. The word "not" is the Greek word *ouk*, which is *an emphatic form of the word "no."* In context here, it means *to emphatically, categorically not know something.* The use of the words *ouk* (not) and *oida* (know) is the equivalent of Paul saying, "Have you guys not gotten it yet? Do you not know by now what race you're supposed to be running?"

Unfortunately, there are many Christians who don't know what race they are called to run, but that doesn't have to be your story. You can know what your race is and run it to win. The word "run" in First Corinthians 9:24 is a translation of the Greek word *trecho,* which means *to run,* but the form here pictures *one who has jumped into the race and is pressing ahead with all his might to reach a goal set before him; one who is running at such a pace that both feet never hit the ground at the same time.* With his eyes fixed on the prize, this runner is steadily moving forward toward the goal.

The word "race" in this verse is the Greek word *stadion,* and it describes *a race course that was 600 feet in length or one eighth of a Roman mile.* It is the same word used to describe the racecourse in Isthmia, not far from the city of Corinth, where the Isthmian Games were held. The word *stadion* is from where we get the word for a *stadium,* a place where athletic competitions were held. Those participating in these games were noted for being disciplined, balanced, and committed to excellence.

The Corinthian believers understood what Paul was trying to communicate through this illustration because they had attended and watched the Isthmian games in Corinth. By using the word *stadion,* Paul was telling the Corinthians — and us — that if we're going to reach our goal and take hold of our prize, we have to be committed, balanced, and determined to be our very best.

Paul went on to say, "…They which run in a race run all…" (1 Corinthians 9:24). The word "all" in Greek is *pantes,* which means *all,* indicating *every single person is in the race.* All of us have been given a specific race to "run." Again, we see the Greek word *trecho* — translated here as "run" —meaning *to jump into the race and press ahead with all one's might to reach the goal set before him.* Distractions are removed, and we are moving so fast that both of our feet never hit the ground at the same time.

Only One Receives the Prize

What else did Paul say about our race? He said that all run, "…but one receiveth the prize" (1 Corinthians 9:24). In Greek, the word "one" is *heis,* meaning *one;* it refers to *one and one only.* In the ancient games, only one person received the prize; there were no trophies given just for participating.

We are living in a time when children are given what is called participation trophies. These are awards given to every child who participates in sporting events but does not finish in first, second, or third place. Normally, only the top three competitors would be eligible for a trophy. But because some worry that losing will affect a child's self-esteem, participation trophies have become the norm. Some professions argue that participation trophies promote narcissism and a sense of entitlement among children. Defenders of participation trophies often argue that these trophies teach children that trying their best is good enough, even if they do not win.

Nevertheless, in God's assessment of things, there are no participation trophies. Only one "receiveth the prize." The word "receiveth" is a translation of the Greek word *lambano*, which means *to seize or to lay hold of something in order to make it your very own* — almost like a person who reaches out to grab, capture, or take possession of something. In some cases, it means *to violently lay hold of something in order to seize and take it as one's very own*. At other times, it depicts *one who graciously receives something that is freely and easily given*.

The word "prize" Paul referred to is the Greek word *brabeion*, which describes *the prizes and rewards given to victors who won in the games; the prize that follows a triumph*. This word also depicts *the umpire, referee, or judge who moderated and judged athletic competitions*. The race official waited at the finish line for the first person to cross the line and then presented him with the award. Again, only one participant received the prize.

So Run That You May Obtain!

Paul wrapped up First Corinthians 9:24 saying, "…So run that ye may obtain." Interestingly, the word "so" in Greek is *houtos*, which means *in this way; in this manner; in line with this; accordingly*. By using this word, Paul was saying, "In the very same way you saw the runners run in the Isthmian Games, run your race in like manner. Remove all distractions, set your eyes on the prize, and give it your very best."

The word "obtain" is the Greek word *katalambano*, which means *to grab hold of; to seize; to wrestle; to pull down; to master and to make your very own*. It pictures *one pouncing, seizing or latching hold of a thing with all of his might*. It also depicts a runner who runs with all his energy to obtain, seize, tackle, conquer, comprehend, overtake, or master the prize. This means if you're going to obtain what God has called you to obtain, you're going to have to give it your very best.

What is God calling you to obtain? Is it to get out of debt and be in a stronger financial position? Is it to be a better wife or husband? Is it to train and raise up godly children who walk with the Lord? Is it to lose weight and become physically fit? Is it to complete your college education and land your dream job? Or is it to build a network of healthy, meaningful relationships?

Whatever God is calling you to do, give yourself to it! One day you will stand before His throne and give an account of what you did in this life. In the moment, nothing will be more rewarding than looking into the eyes of Jesus and saying with confidence, "Lord, I did all I knew to do to finish my race. To the best of my ability, I have obtained everything I knew how to attain."

Friend, it's time to jump into the racecourse God has called you to run, remove all distractions, and move steadily toward the finish line. Run your race that you may obtain the prize! In our next lesson, we will examine the difference between the two types of rewards you can expect to receive from running your race with purpose: temporary and eternal rewards.

STUDY QUESTIONS

Study to shew thyself approved unto God, a workman that needeth not to be ashamed, rightly dividing the word of truth.
— 2 Timothy 2:15

1. Those participating in athletic games were noted for being *disciplined*, *balanced*, and *committed* to excellence. Be honest: Does this describe you? In what area, or areas, of your life do you need to cultivate more discipline? Where are you out of balance? And where do you need to develop greater commitment?

2. According to Paul's words in Philippians 3:8-10, what is the greatest prize we should always be seeking to obtain? (Also consider Psalm 27:4; 73:26; Luke 10:38-42.)

PRACTICAL APPLICATION

But be ye doers of the word, and not hearers only,
deceiving your own selves.
—James 1:22

1. In order for you to successfully "run" (*trecho*) the race God has called you to run, you have *to jump into the race, press ahead with all your might, and totally focus on the goal line — removing all distractions that arise.* What might be distracting you, or possibly trying to derail you, from doing what God has called you to do?

2. What practical steps can you take to lessen or remove this distraction from your life?

3. In your own words, what does it look like to run in such a way as to get the prize?

4. What "prize" or "prizes" are you pressing forward to obtain — what are you trying *to grab hold of; seize; wrestle; pull down; master and make your very own?*

LESSON 3

TOPIC

Temporary and Eternal Rewards

SCRIPTURES

1. **Romans 14:10** — ...For we shall all stand before the judgment seat of Christ.

2. **Romans 8:1** — There is therefore now no condemnation to them which are in Christ Jesus...

3. **Psalm 103:12** — As far as the east is from the west, so far hath he removed our transgressions from us.

4. **Romans 14:12** — So then every one of us shall give an account of himself to God.

5. **2 Corinthians 5:10** — For we must all appear before the judgment seat of Christ; that every one may receive the things done in his body, according to that he hath done, whether it be good or bad.

6. **Ephesians 2:10** — For we are his workmanship, created in Christ Jesus unto good works, which God hath before ordained that we should walk in them.

7. **1 Corinthians 9:24,25** — Know ye not that they which run in a race run all, but one receiveth the prize? So run, that ye may obtain. And every man that striveth for the mastery is temperate in all things. Now they do it to obtain a corruptible crown; but we an incorruptible.

GREEK WORDS

1. "all" — **πάντες** (*pantes*): all, indicating every single person in each race

2. "stand" — **παρίστημι** (*paristemi*): to stand, not crawl or grovel; indicates there will be no shame there whatsoever

3. "judgment seat" — **βῆμα** (*bema*): a platform on which a judge or governor gave a judgment; a place of designation; taken from the ancient Greek Isthmian games in which athletes competed for a reward, and as they competed, they were under the careful scrutiny of judges who watched to make sure every rule of the contest was obeyed; after the games ended, victors were led to a platform, which was called the bema, where a judge placed a laurel crown on the heads of those who had fought well

4. "every one of us shall give an account of himself to God" — **ἕκαστος ἡμῶν περὶ ἑαυτοῦ λόγον δώσει τῷ Θεῷ** (*hekastos hemon peri heautou logon dosei to Theo*): "Every one of us without exception will give a factual, verbal report of himself to God – it will be a full verbal accounting of himself to God."

5. "appear" — **φανερός** (*phaneros*): to appear, to manifest, to become visible; to become apparent; to become seen; to be well known; or to become conspicuous; to become visible, observable, obvious, clear, open, apparent, or evident

6. "before" — **ἔμπροσθεν** (*emprosthen*): right in front of; before the face; face to face

7. "receive" — **κομίζω** (*komidzo*): to receive what is due or what one has coming to him; exactly what one has earned

8. "before ordained" — **προετοιμάζω** (*proetoimadzo*): a compound of **πρό** (*pro*) and ἑτοιμάζω (*hetoimadzo*); the word **πρό** (*pro*) means before, in front of, or before in terms of time; the word ἑτοιμάζω (*hetoimadzo*) means to make ready, prepare: to make the necessary

preparations, get everything ready, full readiness and preparation; compounded, it means to previously do everything necessary to make ready and fully prepared

9. "walk" — περιπατέω (*peripateo*): to walk around, to live and carry on in one general vicinity; pictures a person who has walked on one path or vicinity for so long that he can now almost walk that path blindfolded; suggests one who has walked in one region for so long that it has now become his environment, his place of daily activity; often translated to live; to stroll

10. "prize" — βραβεῖον (*brabeion*): describes the prizes and rewards given to victors who won in the games; the prize that follows a triumph; also depicts the umpire, referee, or judge who moderated and judged athletic competitions

11. "so" — οὕτως (*houtos*): thus; in this way; in this manner; in keeping with; in line with this; accordingly

12. "run" — τρέχω (*trecho*): to run, but the form here pictures one who is running; pictures one who has jumped into the race and is pressing ahead with all his might to reach a goal set before him; one who is running at such a pace that both feet never hit the ground at the same time; with eyes fixed on the finish line, the runner makes a run for it, steadily moving forward toward the goal

13. "obtain" — καταλαμβάνω (*katalambano*): to grab hold of; to seize; to wrestle; to pull down; to master and to make your very own; pictures one pouncing, seizing or latching hold of a thing with all of his might; depicts a runner who runs with all his energy to obtain, seize, tackle, conquer, comprehend, overtake, or master the prize

SYNOPSIS

What do clowns, musicians, and a family circus have in common with teaching the Gospel? You might think, *Nothing at all.* But this is actually Rick's family heritage! Back in the late 1800s his great grandfather, who had been a band director for the legendary P.T. Barnum for two decades, owned a family circus. When he first came to what would be Oklahoma, it wasn't part of the United States yet. As they traveled, they set up their big-top tent and entertained audiences with their animal acts, orchestral pieces, clowns, and novelty sideshows.

According to the world's standards, Rick's family looked like clowns. Yet as unlikely as it seemed, God saw into the future and chose Rick to be a powerful preacher and teacher of God's Word. Indeed, just as the apostle Paul stated, "God hath chosen the foolish things of the world to confound the wise…" (1 Corinthians 1:27).

What about you? Do you know *your* family history? Does it seem unlikely that God could use you to build His Kingdom? If so, then you're likely a perfect candidate to do something extraordinary for His glory. The fact is, God handpicked you — before the world began — to carry out a specific, much-needed assignment. And there are rewards that await you as you fulfill your destiny.

The emphasis of this lesson:

We as believers will stand before the Judgment Seat of Christ and personally give an account of what we did with our lives. Jesus will examine and evaluate each of our works and reward us with exactly what we have earned.

Only Believers Will Stand Before the Judgment Seat of Christ

As we wrapped up Lesson 2, we talked about some of the possible short-term goals God may be calling you to pursue. These may include:

- Getting out of debt and being in a stronger financial position
- Being a better wife or husband
- Training and raising up godly children who walk with the Lord
- Losing weight and becoming physically fit
- Completing your college education and landing your dream job
- Starting your own business
- Building a network of healthy, long-lasting relationships
- Having enough money to be able to retire

Clearly, these are all very noble goals for the here and now, but there are also eternal goals with eternal rewards that are even more valuable. The Bible says, "…For we shall all stand before the judgment seat of Christ" (Romans 14:10). In that moment, when you stand before God and give an account for what you did in this life, nothing will be more rewarding than looking into the eyes of Jesus and saying with confidence, "Lord, I did all I knew to do to finish my race. To the best of my ability, I have obtained everything You placed in my heart."

The good news is, if you're standing before the Judgment Seat of Christ, you have made it into Heaven! You are saved by God's grace and will be with the Lord forever. Unsaved people will not stand before the Judgment Seat of Christ; they will stand before God's White-Throne Judgment, which will take place at the end of Christ's thousand-year (millennial) reign (*see* Revelation 20:11-15).

It is important to understand that the Judgment Seat of Christ is *not* a place where believers will be reprimanded for their past sins. Any person who has repented of their sins has been forgiven (*see* First John 1:9). The blood of Christ has washed away every sin, and God remembers it no more. In fact, the Bible says, "As far as the east is from the west, so far hath he removed our transgressions from us" (Psalm 103:12).

When we repent of our sin and confess that Jesus is the Lord of our life, we immediately become a new creation in Christ; our old life has passed away, and our new life has begun (*see* Second Corinthians 5:17). This brings us to one of the greatest promises penned in Scripture — Romans 8:1, which says, "There is therefore now no condemnation to them which are in Christ Jesus...." Friend, promises like these give us reason to rejoice!

Christ's Judgment Seat
Is Where We'll Receive Our Rewards

You may be thinking, *Well, if God forgives our sins and completely forgets them, why do we stand before the Judgment Seat of Christ?* That's a good question. Looking again at Romans 14:10, it says, "...For we shall all stand before the judgment seat of Christ." Let's take a few minutes to unpack the original Greek meaning of some of the words in this verse.

First, notice the word "all." It is the Greek word *pantes*, which means *all,* and indicates *every single believer without exception.* Therefore, if you're saved, you will stand before Christ's Judgment Seat. Next, notice the word "stand." In Greek, it is the word *paristemi*, and it means *to stand, not crawl or grovel.* The use of this word clearly indicates *there will be no shame there whatsoever.* When you come before Christ, you're going to walk before

His throne with your shoulders back and head held high — not because of anything you have done, but because of what He has done for you. With great appreciation for Christ's sacrifice, you will enter the presence of the King of kings and Lord of lords.

This brings us to the words "judgment seat." Upon hearing the word *judgment*, many people misunderstand what is being said in this verse. In Greek, the words "judgment seat" is the word *bema*, which describes *a platform on which a judge or governor gave a judgment or reward*. It was a place of designation taken from the ancient Greek Isthmian games where athletes competed for a reward. And as they competed, they were under the careful scrutiny of judges who watched to make sure every rule of the contest was obeyed. After the games ended, victors were led to a platform, which was called the *bema*, where a judge placed a laurel crown on the heads of those who had fought well.

The use of this word tells us that we are in a spiritual race that requires us to give our very best and fight to win. And just as the winning athletes appeared before the *bema* to receive awards from a human governor, one day we'll stand before the *bema* of Christ, and He'll reward us based on how well we ran our race. Again, the *bema* (Judgment Seat) of Christ is not a place where losers are punished. It's a place where we as believers will receive rewards based on how well we carried out our assignment.

This is why it's truly crucial for you to know your divine purpose and walk in it. In other words, you need to know what specific race God has called you to run and understand the primary goal He wants you to obtain with your life.

Every Believer Will Give An Account of Himself to God

Just two verses later, Paul went on to say, "So then every one of us shall give an account of himself to God" (Romans 14:12). This is a very sobering statement. In fact, when you read it in Greek it's even stronger. The word "everyone" is the Greek word *hekastos*, which means *every one of us without exception*. Hence, no one can avoid this moment — if you're a Christian, this day awaits you in your future.

The Bible says, "So then every one of us (*hekastos* — every one of us without exception) shall give an account of himself to God" (Romans

14:12). In Greek, the phrase "shall give" is the word *dosei*, which means *will personally deliver* or *personally give* to God. The word *account* is the Greek word *logon*, which in this verse describes *a factual report*.

Taking into account the original Greek meanings of these words, here is the *Renner Interpretive Version (RIV)* of Romans 14:12:

> **Every one of us without exception will give a factual, verbal report of himself to God — it will be a full verbal accounting of himself to God.**

This factual, verbal report of all our activities will be personally given to God by each of us when we stand at the *bema* (Judgment Seat) of Christ. Again, Jesus will not be there as a judge to examine what we did wrong; He will sit and determine our rewards for what we did right.

When the apostle Paul came to the end of his life and he was about to enter into eternity, he said, "I have fought a good fight, I have finished my course, I have kept the faith: henceforth there is laid up for me a crown of righteousness, which the Lord, the righteous judge, shall give me at that day..." (2 Timothy 4:7,8). Clearly, there is no fear in Paul's words. He was ready to look into the eyes of Jesus and confidently say that he had done his very best to run the race he had been given.

We Will Receive Exactly What We Have Earned

The revelation of our standing before Jesus to give an account for our lives was deeply rooted in Paul's heart. We see this concept appear in multiple places throughout his New Testament writings, including Second Corinthians 5:10, which says, "For we must all appear before the judgment seat of Christ; that every one may receive the things done in his body, according to that he hath done, whether it be good or bad."

Once more he uses the Greek word *hekastos* — translated here as "all" — which is an all-inclusive word that literally means *every single person, no one excluded*. If you are a child of God, you are going to "...appear before the judgment seat of Christ...." The word "appear" is the Greek word *phaneros*, and it means *to appear, to manifest*, or *to become visible*. It carries the idea of *becoming visible, observable, obvious, clear, open, apparent, or evident*. Moreover, it means *to become apparent; to become seen; to be well known*; or *to become conspicuous*. The fact that the Holy Spirit prompted

Paul to use this word tells us that in the moment we stand before Christ, all things about our lives will be made clear.

Interestingly, even the word "before" is important. It is the Greek word *emprosthen*, which means *right in front of, before the face, face to face*. In that moment, we are going to be *right in front of* Jesus, looking at Him *face to face*. And each of us will "…receive the things done in his body…" (2 Corinthians 5:10). In Greek, the word "receive" is *komidzo*, which means *to receive what is due* or *what one has coming to him*; to receive *exactly what one has earned*.

Again, this time before the Judgment Seat of Christ is not at all calling our salvation into question. Anyone who stands before the *bema* of Christ is saved and in Heaven. This divine moment before Jesus is an evaluation of your life's work to determine exactly what rewards you have coming to you. How did you run your race? Did you half-heartedly serve the Lord, or did you give it your all and obtain what God called you to pursue?

We Are Created for Good Works

This takes us back to Ephesians 2:10, which says, "For we are his workmanship, created in Christ Jesus unto good works, which God hath before ordained that we should walk in them." The phrase "before ordained" is a translation of the Greek word *proetoimadzo*, a compound of the words *pro* and *hetoimadzo*. The word *pro* means *before, in front of*, or *before in terms of time*; the word *hetoimadzo* means *to make ready or prepare: to make the necessary preparations, get everything ready, full readiness and preparation*. When these words are compounded to form the word *proetoimadzo*, it means *to previously do everything necessary to make ready and fully prepared*. The inclusion of this word lets us know that God has a specific, tailor-made plan for each and every one of us, and that we're fully equipped to carry it out.

Furthermore, God fully intends for us to walk in His plan and do the good works He has preplanned for us. The word "walk" in Greek is *peripateo*, which means *to walk around or to live and carry on in one general vicinity*. It pictures *a person who has walked on one path or vicinity for so long that he can now almost walk that path blindfolded*. It suggests *one who has walked in one region for so long that it has now become his environment, his place of daily activity*. Oftentimes, the word *peripateo* is translated *to live* or *to stroll*.

Make no mistake: before the foundation of the world, God established a specific race course just for you to run. He designed it with you in mind, and His intention is for you to move into that customized place and live there. As you continue to stroll daily in the race He's called you to, there are many temporary rewards you will receive along the way. But most importantly, when you finish your race and look into Jesus' face, there will be no greater reward than the eternal satisfaction of knowing that you gave it your very best and to hear the words, "Well done, my good and faithful servant."

STUDY QUESTIONS

Study to shew thyself approved unto God, a workman that needeth
not to be ashamed, rightly dividing the word of truth.
— 2 Timothy 2:15

1. Prior to the lesson, had you ever heard of the "Judgment Seat of Christ"? If so, what was your understanding of it? What did this lesson show you that you hadn't seen before? How has it changed your perspective of what this experience will be like?

2. Now that you know that you will one day stand before Jesus and give an account for your life, how will that affect your day-to-day living? What do you think you would stop doing? What do you think you will start doing? (Consider Galatians 6:9,10; Ephesians 5:14-17.)

PRACTICAL APPLICATION

But be ye doers of the word, and not hearers only,
deceiving your own selves.
— James 1:22

1. What are some of your short-term goals? What are some of the things you hope to accomplish in the next few years? What practical steps are you taking to see these goals become reality?

2. What are some of your long-term goals? What are some of the hopes and dreams that God has placed in your heart that you want to see come to pass before you leave this life?

3. What promises in God's Word come to mind that connect with your goals?

TOPIC

What Is Your Strategy To Reach Your Goal?

SCRIPTURES

1. **1 Corinthians 9:24-26** — Know ye not that they which run in a race run all, but one receiveth the prize? So run, that ye may obtain. And every man that striveth for the mastery is temperate in all things. Now they do it to obtain a corruptible crown; but we an incorruptible. I therefore so run, not as uncertainly; so fight I, not as one that beateth the air.

2. **2 Corinthians 10:4** — For the weapons of our warfare are not carnal, but mighty through God to the pulling down of strong holds.

GREEK WORDS

1. "know" — **οἶδα** (*oida*): to see, perceive, understand, or comprehend

2. "not" — **οὐκ** (*ouk*): an emphatic form of "no"; emphatically, categorically not

3. "run" — **τρέχω** (*trecho*): to run, but the form here pictures one who is running; pictures one who has jumped into the race and is pressing ahead with all his might to reach a goal set before him; one who is running at such a pace that both feet never hit the ground at the same time; with eyes fixed on the finish line, the runner makes a run for it, steadily moving forward toward the goal

4. "race" — **στάδιον** (*stadion*): a race course that was 600 feet in length or one-eighth of a Roman mile, the exact length used in the Olympics of the ancient world and in the Isthmian Games held near the city of Corinth; it eventually became the word for a stadium, a place where athletic competitions were held; those participating in these games were noted for being disciplined, balanced, and committed to excellence

5. "all" — **πάντες** (*pantes*): all, indicating every single person in each race

6. "one" — **εἷς** (*heis*): one; refers to one and one only

7. "receiveth" — λαμβάνω (*lambano*): to seize or to lay hold of something in order to make it your very own, almost like a person who reaches out to grab, capture, or take possession of something; in some cases, it means to violently lay hold of something in order to seize and take it as one's very own; at other times, it depicts one who graciously receives something that is freely and easily given

8. "prize" — βραβεῖον (*brabeion*): describes the prizes and rewards given to victors who won in the games; the prize that follows a triumph; also depicts the umpire, referee, or judge who moderated and judged athletic competitions

9. "so" — οὕτως (*houtos*): in this way; in this manner; in line with this; accordingly

10. "obtain" — καταλαμβάνω (*katalambano*): to grab hold of; to seize; to wrestle; to pull down; to master and to make your very own; pictures one pouncing, seizing or latching hold of a thing with all of his might; depicts a runner who runs with all his energy to obtain, seize, tackle, conquer, comprehend, overtake, or master the prize

11. "every man" — πᾶς (*pas*): all, everyone running in a race

12. "striveth for the mastery" — ἀγωνίζομαι (*agonidzomai*): agony; tense depicts a continuous agony, hence agonizing; depicts an intense conflict or contest; a struggle; a fight; great exertion or effort; often used to convey the ideas of anguish, pain, distress, and conflict; it comes from the word ἀγών (*agon*) which depicts the athletic conflicts and competitions that were so famous in the ancient world; frequently pictures wrestlers in a wrestling match, with each wrestler struggling with all his might to overcome his opponent in an effort to hurl him to the ground in a fight to the finish; used figuratively to describe a struggle of the human will

13. "temperate" — ἐγκρατεύομαι (*enkrateuomai*): to be in control; denotes power over one's self; to exercise self-dominion; often translated as self-control; it suggests the control or restraint of one's passions, appetites, and desires; restraint, moderation, discipline, balance, temperance, or self-control; listed as a fruit of the Spirit in Galatians 5:23

14. "all things" — πάντα (*panta*): all things; everything, even the smallest details

15. "corruptible" — φθαρτός (*phthartos*): perishable; corruptible; temporary; not long lasting; something that is capable of decay; that which

is capable of suffering the effects of wear, tear, and age; destructible; that which eventually breaks down

16. "crown" — στέφανος (*stephanos*): a victor's crown; in ancient games, a laurel wreath was placed on the head of winning athletes; athletes who obtained a victor's crown were esteemed and honored the rest of their lives; memories of his achievement were etched into society an ensured that he would not be overlooked or forgotten during the balance of life; the word could be used in reference to any type of reward

17. "incorruptible" — ἄφθαρτος (*aphthartos*): something that is incapable of decay; that which is incapable of suffering the effects of wear, tear, and age; timeless, immortal, indestructible

18. "warfare" — στρατεία (*strateia*): where we get the word strategy

19. "I" — ἐγώ (*ego*): emphatically "I"; Paul uses this personal pronoun to make himself his chief example

20. "therefore" — τοίνυν (*toinun*): accordingly; therefore; indeed right now; in light of what I have said, this is my logical response that is now required

21. "uncertainly" — αδήλως (*adelos*): uncertainly; aimlessly; without direction; having no plan; no aim

SYNOPSIS

In Ephesians 6:16, the apostle Paul wrote, "Above all, taking the shield of faith, wherewith ye shall be able to quench all the fiery darts of the wicked." In this verse, the words "above all" are a translation of the Greek phrase *epi pasin*, which means *out in front of all* or *covering all*. It describes the *position* of one's faith — it is not something that is behind us or off to the side. Our faith acts like a shield that is *out in front of us, covering every part of us.*

Having been chained to a Roman soldier for nearly two years, Paul was very familiar with the Roman shield. It was actually the size of a door and was both tall and wide. It covered the soldier from head to foot, side to side. Paul compared our faith with the Roman shield to let us know that our faith — when used correctly — should be out in front of us, covering us from head to toe. When our faith is in place, we are protected from the fiery darts of the enemy and able to move forward in the race God has called us to run. Indeed, utilizing our shield of faith is a big part of God's strategy to experience victory.

The emphasis of this lesson:

In order to obtain the eternal rewards God has for us, we must 'strive for the mastery' and be 'temperate in all things.' This means we will experience agonizing moments when we struggle with our flesh. But if we exercise self-control over our passions and desires, we will make it to the end and win our race.

A Review of Our Anchor Verse
First Corinthians 9:24

In our previous lessons, we noted that the city of Corinth was just a few miles from Isthmia, the city where the great Isthmian games occurred once every two years. Because Corinth was so close to Isthmia, the Corinthians went there by the thousands to watch all the contests, including the footraces. Paul knew this, and therefore used the illustration of a footrace to communicate truth to the Corinthian believers.

Every Believer Is in a Race

In First Corinthians 9:24, he said, "Know ye not that they which run in a race run all, but one receiveth the prize? So run, that ye may obtain." We have seen that the word "know" here is the Greek word *oida*, which means *to see, perceive, understand, or comprehend.* The word "not" in Greek is *ouk*, which is *an emphatic form of the word "no."* When we couple together the words *oida* and *ouk* (know not) in the context of this verse, it is almost as if Paul was saying, "What is wrong with you all? After all the footraces you've watched in Isthmia, have you not yet comprehended that when people jump in the race, they put everything they have into running it?"

The word "run" is from the Greek word *trecho*, which means *to run*, but the form here pictures *one who is in the process of running.* It pictures *one who has jumped into the race and is pressing ahead with all his might to reach a goal set before him.* This person is running at such a pace that both feet never hit the ground at the same time. With his eyes fixed on the finish line, he makes a run for it, steadily moving forward toward the goal.

This brings us to the word "race" — the Greek word *stadion*. This word described *a race course that was 600 feet in length or one-eighth of a Roman mile*, the exact length used in the Olympics of the ancient world and in the Isthmian Games held near the city of Corinth. Eventually, the word *stadion* became the word for a *stadium*, a place where athletic competitions were held. Those participating in these games were noted for being disciplined, balanced, and committed to excellence. By using this word, Paul was telling believers, "If you're going to finish your race, you're going to need to be disciplined, balanced, and committed to excellence, or you'll never make it to the end."

God Wants Us To Receive the Prize

Paul said that as believers we "all" run in a race, "…but one receiveth the prize…" (1 Corinthians 9:24). The word "all" is the Greek word *pantes* which means *all*, indicating *every single person in each race*. The word "one" in Greek is *heis*, meaning *one and one only*. Each and every one of us is running in various spiritual races, and Paul is urging us to run in such a way that we want to finish first. Mentally, emotionally, physically, and spiritually, we need to put forth the effort to be number one at whatever we are called to do so that we will "receiveth the prize."

In Greek, the word "receiveth" is the word *lambano*, and it means *to seize or to lay hold of something in order to make it your very own, almost like a person who reaches out to grab, capture, or take possession of something*. In some cases, *lambano* means *to violently lay hold of something in order to seize and take it as one's very own*. At other times, it depicts *one who graciously receives something that is freely and easily given*. This word is quite fitting when it comes to describing our interaction with God. He freely and graciously gives us everything we need to live the Christian life (*see* Second Peter 1:3), but in order for His provisions to become a reality in our lives, we must develop the mentality to reach out in faith to *seize them and take them and make them our very own*.

When we run our race to take first place, the Bible says we will receive the "prize." This is the Greek word *brabeion*, and it describes *the prizes and rewards given to victors who won in the games* or *the prize that follows a triumph*. This word was also used to depict *the umpire, referee, or judge who moderated and judged athletic competitions and who awarded the winners by placing laurel crowns on their heads*.

In our case, Jesus is standing at the end of our race as the umpire, the referee, and the judge of the games. He is waiting for us to cross the finish line so that He can place a crown of victory on our heads. Realizing that He is at the finish line cheering us on is a great motivator to keep pressing on when times get tough and we grow tired and want to quit.

So Run That You May Obtain It

With this in mind, Paul added, "…So run, that ye may obtain" (1 Corinthians 9:24). The word "so" is the Greek word *houtos*, which means *in this way*, *in this manner*, or *in line with this*. Paul's use of this word here tells his readers, "*In the exact same manner* as the athletes run their races in the Isthmian Games, you are to run your spiritual race. Focus on the finish line and run (*trecho*) — move your feet so fast that they never hit the ground at the same time. Remove all distractions from your field of vision and fix your eyes on Jesus who is on His feet at the end of the race cheering you on and waiting to reward you with an amazing prize."

If we run in this way, we will "obtain" the prize. The word "obtain" is a translation of the Greek word *katalambano*, which is a compound of the words *kata* and *lambano*. The word *kata* carries the idea of *domination* or *subjugation*, and the word *lambano* means *to take* or *to receive*. When these two words are compounded to form the new word *katalambano*, it means *to grab hold of*, *to seize*, *to wrestle*, *to pull down*, *to master and to make your very own*. It pictures *one pouncing, seizing or latching hold of a thing with all of his might*. Here it depicts *a runner who runs with all his energy to obtain, seize, tackle, conquer, comprehend, overtake, or master the prize*. That is the attitude you need to have in order to make it all the way to the end.

'Strive for the Mastery'

In First Corinthians 9:25, Paul went on to say, "And every man that striveth for the mastery is temperate in all things. Now they do it to obtain a corruptible crown; but we an incorruptible." Notice the phrase "striveth for the mastery." It is a translation of the Greek word *agonidzomai*, which is from where we get the word *agony*. It comes from the word *agon*, which depicts *the athletic conflicts and competitions that were so famous in the ancient world*. This word was frequently used to picture wrestlers in a wrestling match, with each wrestler struggling with all his might to overcome his opponent in an effort to hurl him to the ground in a fight to the finish. Figuratively, this word describes a struggle of the human will.

It should be noted that the tense of the word *agonidzomai* — translated here as "striveth for the mastery" — depicts *one in a continuous agony*, hence *agonizing*. It depicts *an intense conflict or contest*; *a struggle*; *a fight*; *great exertion or effort*. This word was often used to convey the ideas of *anguish, pain, distress, and conflict*. It is the same word used to describe what Jesus Himself experienced in the Garden of Gethsemane. The Bible says He was in "agony" (*see* Luke 22:44) just before He was scourged and crucified on the Cross. But He endured it all through the power of the Holy Spirit and won His race!

It is important to understand that there will be some things you go through in your Christian walk that will be agonizing. Your flesh is going to be screaming, "This is too hard! Go another way!" or "I can't take this anymore. Give up!" But don't listen to it. Through the power of the Holy Spirit, learn to crucify your flesh and keep pressing forward to finish the race Christ has called you to run.

Be 'Temperate in All Things'

Paul said, "And every man that striveth for the mastery is temperate in all things..." (1 Corinthians 9:25). The word "temperate" is the Greek word *enkrateuomai*, which means *to be in control*. It denotes *power over one's self* or *to exercise self-dominion*. It is often translated as *self-control*, and it suggests *the control or restraint of one's passions, appetites, and desires*. Furthermore, it describes *restraint, moderation, discipline, balance, temperance, or self-control*. It is listed as a fruit of the Spirit in Galatians 5:23.

Thus, the Bible says you are to exercise self-dominion or self-control over yourself in "all things." In Greek, the phrase "all things" is the word *panta*, and it describes *all things; everything, even the smallest details*. This clearly lets us know that in order to successfully run the race marked out for us, we are going to have to exercise restraint and discipline in every area of our lives.

If you fail to exercise restraint, your flesh will eventually knock you out of the race. The Bible says, "Just as Death and Destruction are never satisfied, so human desire is never satisfied" (Proverbs 27:20 *NLT*). Thankfully, the Bible also says, "...Let the Holy Spirit guide your lives. Then you won't be doing what your sinful nature craves" (Galatians 5:16 *NLT*). As you surrender yourself daily and obey the promptings of the Holy Spirit, He will develop the fruit of self-control in you.

Secure God's Winning Strategy

The apostle Paul concluded First Corinthians 9:25 by saying, "...Now they do it to obtain a corruptible crown; but we an incorruptible." What's interesting is that athletes competing in the games went through all their preparation and training for a *temporary* reward — a wreath of flowers that quickly faded and died. However, as believers, all our preparation and training will one day produce *eternal* rewards.

This brings us to a very important question that we all need to ask ourselves: What is our strategy for getting from where we are to the end of our race in eternity? The truth is we are in a spiritual war. The Bible says, "For we wrestle not against flesh and blood, but against principalities, against powers, against the rulers of the darkness of this world, against spiritual wickedness in high places" (Ephesians 6:12).

The only way to win a spiritual war is to fight spiritually, using spiritual weapons. Paul said, "For the weapons of our warfare are not carnal, but mighty through God to the pulling down of strong holds" (2 Corinthians 10:4). The word "warfare" in this verse is the Greek word *strateia*, which is from where we get the word *strategy*. This tells us that we are up against an invisible enemy who methodically and cautiously charts out a strategic assault against us.

Thankfully, the word *strateia* doesn't just describe Satan's strategies. It also tells us that God has a strategy too — one that is far superior. If we will seek God and listen to the voice of the Holy Spirit, He will give us the divine strategy we need to defeat the devil. The Holy Spirit knows everything, and He will lead and guide you into all truth if you seek Him! (*See* John 16:13.)

What was Paul's strategy to finish his race? Part of it is recorded in First Corinthians 9:26, which says, "I therefore so run, not as uncertainly; so fight I, not as one that beateth the air." Paul said he didn't run "uncertainly," which in Greek means *uncertainly; aimlessly; without direction; having no plan; no aim.* This word is the picture of a runner who is planning to run in a race, but he has no idea where the race course is. He just goes out and begins running aimlessly, exerting all kinds of energy running this way and that way, but because he has no strategy, he never gets anywhere.

Does this describe your journey with God? Are you aimlessly running here and there and getting nowhere fast? It doesn't have to be that way. God wants to give you the winning strategy you need to run your race in order for you to obtain the prize He has waiting for you. His Spirit sees all and knows all and is waiting for you to be still and open your ears so He can tell you what you need to know.

In our final lesson, we will continue to explore the meaning of First Corinthians 9:27 and learn what we need to do to avoid the dangers of becoming a "castaway."

STUDY QUESTIONS

> Study to shew thyself approved unto God, a workman that needeth
> not to be ashamed, rightly dividing the word of truth.
> — 2 Timothy 2:15

1. In the Garden of Gethsemane, Jesus was in such agony of soul that He sweat great drops of blood (*see* Luke 22:44). Yet there was something about His focus that helped Him endure it all. According to Hebrews 12:2-4, where were His eyes fixed? What does this passage instruct you to do when you're in agony and overwhelmed by the circumstances of life?

2. Through Paul, God instructs us to be "temperate in all things" (*see* 1 Corinthians 9:25). What does temperance look like? Read Romans 13:12 and 13; Galatians 5:24; Ephesians 4:22; and Colossians 3:5-10 and describe what it means to be temperate.

3. Would you like to know the secrets to living a temperate life? God reveals them in His Word. Take time to read these verses and identify three primary keys to living victoriously.

   • Romans 12:1; Galatians 2:20; Colossians 3:3; 1 Corinthians 15:31

   • Romans 8:13; Galatians 5:16,25

   • Romans 13:14; Colossians 3:1-3,12; 1 Peter 5:5

4. The Bible says that Jesus was flesh and blood just like us and was tempted in every way — yet He did not sin (*see* Hebrews 4:15). Why was it necessary for Him to become fully human? And how does His humanity help us through our struggles? (Consider Hebrews 2:14-18 and Hebrews 4:15,16 as you answer.)

PRACTICAL APPLICATION

> But be ye doers of the word, and not hearers only,
> deceiving your own selves.
> — James 1:22

1. There are great eternal rewards that Jesus has set aside just for you if you finish your race. The question is: What is your strategy for reaching your goal? What are your short-term and long-term plans for completing the assignments God gave you?

2. Are you aimlessly running around and getting nowhere fast? God wants to put an end to your exhaustion and give you the strategy you need to run your race successfully. Take time now to be still and acknowledge that Jesus is the Lord of your life. Repent of anything that stands between you and Him, such as pride or unconfessed sin. Ask the Holy Spirit for the direction you need at this present season in life — and then listen. What is He saying to you?

LESSON 5

TOPIC
What Is a Castaway?

SCRIPTURES

1. **1 Corinthians 9:24-27** — Know ye not that they which run in a race run all, but one receiveth the prize? So run, that ye may obtain; and every man that striveth for the mastery is temperate in all things. Now they do it to obtain a corruptible crown; but we an incorruptible. I therefore so run, not as uncertainly; so fight I, not as one that beateth the air. But I keep under my body, and bring it into subjection: lest that by any means, when I have preached to others, I myself should be a castaway

GREEK WORDS

1. "know" — οἶδα (*oida*): to see, perceive, understand, or comprehend

2. "not" — οὐκ (*ouk*): an emphatic form of "no"; emphatically, categorically not

3. "run" — τρέχω (*trecho*): to run, but the form here pictures one who is running; pictures one who has jumped into the race and is pressing ahead with all his might to reach a goal set before him; one who is running at such a pace that both feet never hit the ground at the same

time; with eyes fixed on the finish line, the runner makes a run for it, steadily moving forward toward the goal

4. "race" — στάδιον (*stadion*): a race course that was 600 feet in length or one-eighth of a Roman mile, the exact length used in the Olympics of the ancient world and in the Isthmian Games held near the city of Corinth; it eventually became the word for a stadium, a place where athletic competitions were held; those participating in these games were noted for being disciplined, balanced, and committed to excellence

5. "all" — πάντες (*pantes*): all, indicating every single person in each race

6. "one" — εἷς (*heis*): one; refers to one and one only

7. "receiveth" — λαμβάνω (*lambano*): to seize or to lay hold of something in order to make it your very own, almost like a person who reaches out to grab, capture, or take possession of something; in some cases, it means to violently lay hold of something in order to seize and take it as one's very own; at other times, it depicts one who graciously receives something that is freely and easily given

8. "prize" — βραβεῖον (*brabeion*): describes the prizes and rewards given to victors who won in the games; the prize that follows a triumph; also depicts the umpire, referee, or judge who moderated and judged athletic competitions

9. "every man" — πᾶς (*pas*): all, everyone running in a race

10. "striveth for the mastery" — ἀγωνίζομαι (*agonidzomai*): agony; tense depicts a continuous agony, hence agonizing; depicts an intense conflict or contest; a struggle; a fight; great exertion or effort; often used to convey the ideas of anguish, pain, distress, and conflict; it comes from the word ἀγών (*agon*) which depicts the athletic conflicts and competitions that were so famous in the ancient world; frequently pictures wrestlers in a wrestling match, with each wrestler struggling with all his might to overcome his opponent in an effort to hurl him to the ground in a fight to the finish; used figuratively to describe a struggle of the human will

11. "temperate" — ἐγκρατεύομαι (*enkrateuomai*): to be in control; denotes power over one's self; to exercise self-dominion; often translated as self-control; it suggests the control or restraint of one's passions, appetites, and desires; restraint, moderation, discipline, balance, temperance, or self-control; listed as a fruit of the Spirit in Galatians 5:23

12. "all things" — πάντα (*panta*): all things; everything, even the smallest details

13. "corruptible" — φθαρτός (*phthartos*): perishable; corruptible; temporary; not long lasting; something that is capable of decay; that which is capable of suffering the effects of wear, tear, and age; destructible; that which eventually breaks down

14. "incorruptible" — ἄφθαρτος (*aphthartos*): something that is incapable of decay; that which is incapable of suffering the effects of wear, tear, and age; timeless, immortal, indestructible

15. "I" — ἐγώ (*ego*): emphatically "I"; Paul uses this personal pronoun to make himself his chief example

16. "uncertainly" — αδήλως (*adelos*): uncertainly; aimlessly; without direction; having no plan; no aim

17. "fight I" — πυκτεύω (*pukteuo*): pictures a boxer; used only here in the New Testament

18. "beateth" — δέρω (*dero*): pictures the grueling and barbaric practice of beating someone

19. "air" — ἀήρ (*aer*): the lower, denser regions of the earth's atmosphere; an empty space

20. "I keep under" — ὑπωπιάζω (*hupopiadzo*): to severely strike the lower part of the face below the eyes; to beat where the mouth is located

21. "bring it into subjection" — δουλαγωγέω (*doulagogeo*): to lead about as a slave; to treat as a slave; to subject to stern and rigid discipline: to keep under control or mastery; to dominate; to claim as one's slave

22. "should become" — γίνομαι (*ginomai*): in this case, depicts something that develops progressively and then suddenly overcomes one and takes him off-guard

23. "castaway" — ἀδόκιμος (*adokimos*): no longer approved; unfit; rejected; one who is disapproved, discredited, or disqualified; one who is discredited, dishonored, and shamed; hence, a castaway

SYNOPSIS

One of the pieces of the armor of God He has given us to wear are the shoes of peace (*see* Ephesians 6:15). When Paul wrote about these shoes, he had the shoes of a Roman soldier in mind. On the bottom of these shoes there were one-to-two inch hobnails. These sharp, dagger like spikes enabled soldiers to stand virtually immovable in battle and stomp on anyone who got in their way as they marched forward. Indeed, these were "killer shoes"!

Spiritually speaking, God has given you killer shoes to run your race. Oftentimes, when you begin to make progress in what God has called you to do, the devil rises up to stand in your way. But if you're wearing your shoes of peace, just keep walking! "And the God of peace shall bruise Satan under your feet shortly..." (Romans 16:20). In other words, if the devil is dumb enough to get in front of you, just keep marching forward in God's peace, and crush the enemy under your feet as you forge ahead to accomplish God's will.

The emphasis of this lesson:

A castaway is a person who is no longer approved. They are unfit, rejected, discredited, and disqualified. To keep yourself from being dishonored and shamed in this way, learn to master your flesh — especially the words coming out of your mouth.

A Final Review of Our Anchor Verse
First Corinthians 9:24

As we have seen, Isthmia was a relatively small town located just a few miles from the city of Corinth. It was the home of the great Isthmian Games, which occurred once every two years, and when the games were played, thousands upon thousands of sports lovers flooded the city to watch — including many of the Corinthians. Of all the events, footraces were the most popular. With this in mind, the apostle Paul used the illustration of a footrace to teach them the importance of running the spiritual race God had called them to run. In First Corinthians 9:24, he said:

> **Know ye not that they which run in a race run all, but one receiveth the prize? So run, that ye may obtain.**

The word "know" in this verse is the Greek word *oida*, which means *to see, perceive, understand, or comprehend.* The word "not" in Greek is *ouk*, which is *an emphatic form of the word "no."* When the words *oida* and *ouk* are joined (know ye not), it is the equivalent of Paul saying, "Have you all not comprehended this yet? What's wrong with you? With all the footraces you've seen in Isthmia, have you not yet understood that when people jump in the race, they put everything they have into running it?"

The word "run" is a form of the Greek word *trecho*, which means *to run*, but the form here pictures *one who is running*. It pictures *one who has jumped into the race and is pressing ahead with all his might to reach a goal set before him*. This runner is moving at such a pace that both feet never hit the ground at the same time. His eyes are fixed on the finish line, and he is steadily running and moving forward toward the goal.

The word "race" in this verse is the Greek word *stadion*, and it describes *a race course that was 600 feet in length or one-eighth of a Roman mile*, the exact length used in the Olympics of the ancient world and in the Isthmian Games. The word *stadion* is where we get the word *stadium*. Athletes who participated in these games were known for being disciplined, balanced, and committed to excellence. By using this word, Paul was telling believers, "If you're going to finish your race and make it all the way to the end, there are some specific things that are required: discipline, balance, and commitment to excellence."

Paul noted that as believers, we "all" run in a race. In Greek, the word "all" is the word *pantes*, which indicates *every single person in each race* — including you. You are not here by accident. God chose you from the foundation of the world for a special purpose. Through Paul, He is urging you to run in such a way that you "receiveth the prize."

The word "receiveth" is the Greek word *lambano*, which means *to seize or to lay hold of something in order to make it your very own, almost like a person who reaches out to grab, capture, or take possession of something*. In some cases, *lambano* means *to violently lay hold of something in order to seize and take it as one's very own*. At other times, it depicts *one who graciously receives something that is freely and easily given*. If you think about it, God gives us everything we need, but we must actively take it into our lives. For example, He gave Joshua and the people of Israel the Promised Land, but they had to walk through the entire region and actively *seize the land and make it their very own* (*see* Joshua 1:2-4).

First Corinthians 9:24 concludes, "...But one receiveth the prize? So run, that ye may obtain."

The word "so" is the Greek word *houtos*, which means *in this way; in this manner;* or *in line with this*. Paul used this word to tell his readers, "*In the exact same way* that athletes run their races in the Isthmian Games, you are to run your spiritual race. Focus on the finish line and run (*trecho*) — remove all distractions and move your feet so fast that they never hit the ground at the same time. Fix your eyes on Jesus! He is at the end of the race cheering you on and waiting to reward you with an amazing prize."

The word "prize" is the Greek word *brabeion*, and it describes *the prizes and rewards given to victors who won in the games*. It was also the word used to depict *the umpire, referee, or judge who moderated and judged athletic competitions and who awarded the winners by placing laurel crowns on their heads*. In our case, Jesus is our umpire, our referee, and our judge standing at the finish line waiting to reward us. He is saying, "Don't stop! Don't give up! Just keep coming towards Me because I have something to give you."

Learn To Exercise Self-Control

In the next verse, Paul went on to say, "And every man that striveth for the mastery is temperate in all things..." (1 Corinthians 9:25). In Lesson 4, we learned that the phrase "striveth for the mastery" is a translation of the Greek word *agonidzomai*, which is where we get the word *agony*. The tense of this word describes *one in a continuous agony*, hence *agonizing*. It depicts *an intense conflict or contest; a struggle; a fight; great exertion or effort*. This word was often used to convey the ideas of *anguish, pain, distress, and conflict*. It is the same word used to describe the agony Jesus experienced in the Garden of Gethsemane (*see* Luke 22:44).

The word *agonidzomai* comes from the word *agon*, which depicts *the athletic conflicts and competitions that were so famous in the ancient world*. It was often used to picture wrestlers in a wrestling match, with each wrestler struggling with all his might to overcome his opponent in an effort to hurl him to the ground in a fight to the finish. Figuratively, this word describes *a struggle of the human will*.

The fact is, in order for you to make it to the end of your race and finish the assignments God has given you, you need to conquer "you." That is, you're going to have to wrestle with your flesh — which is your old, carnal nature — and sometimes it is going to be an agonizing experience. The Bible says, "For the desires of the flesh are opposed to the [Holy] Spirit, and the [desires of the] Spirit are opposed to the flesh (godless human nature); for these are antagonistic to each other [continually withstanding and in conflict with each other]..." (Galatians 5:17 *AMPC*).

Nevertheless, if you will learn to be "temperate in all things," you will effectively conquer your flesh. The word "temperate" in First Corinthians 9:25 is the Greek word *enkrateuomai*, which means *to be in control*. It denotes *power over one's self* or *to exercise self-dominion*. It is often translated as *self-control*, and it indicates *the control or restraint of one's passions, appetites, and desires.*

Furthermore, the phrase "all things" is the Greek word *panta*, and it describes *all things; everything, even the smallest details.* The meanings of all these words clearly lets us know that in order to successfully run the race marked out for us, we're going to have to exercise restraint and discipline in every area of our lives. If you allow an area of your flesh to run wild and unrestrained, it can throw you out of your race. Remember, to be victorious, you have to be disciplined, balanced and committed.

Paul Knew Exactly What He Was Aiming for and So Should We

In the second part of First Corinthians 9:25, Paul tells *why* we are to strive for the mastery and be temperate in all things. He said that runners "…do it to obtain a corruptible crown; but we an incorruptible." The word "corruptible" in Greek is *phthartos*, and it describes *something perishable; corruptible; temporary; not long-lasting.* This is the type of reward that natural athletes prepare and compete for. Not us. As believers, we prepare and discipline ourselves to obtain "incorruptible" rewards, which in Greek describes *something that is incapable of decay; that which is incapable of suffering the effects of wear, tear, and age.* It is *timeless, immortal, and indestructible.*

As Paul continues his address in First Corinthians 9:26, he uses himself as an illustration to make his point. He said, "I therefore so run, not as uncertainly…." The word "I" is the Greek word *ego*, which emphatically means *I*. Paul used this personal pronoun to draw attention to himself and make himself the chief example. He basically said, "I'm not just telling you what to do; I'm telling you *this is what I do.* I need to do exactly what I'm telling you to do."

Paul said, "I therefore so run…." Once more, we see the word "run" — from the Greek word *trecho*, describing, *one that is in the process of running, moving their feet as fast as they can, steadily moving toward the finish line.* To this Paul added, "…not as uncertainly…" (1 Corinthians 9:26). The word *not* is again the Greek word *ouk*, which is *the emphatic form of the word no*; and the word "uncertainly" is the Greek word *adelos*, which means *uncertainly, aimlessly, without direction; having no plan; no aim.* Basically, Paul said, "I'm [emphatically] not wasting my time and energy, running aimlessly this way and that way. I'm running with purpose and expending my energy in a specific direction."

To all this, Paul added, "…So fight I, not as one that beateth the air" (1 Corinthians 9:26). In Greek, the phrase "fight I" is *pukteuo*, and it is the word for *a shadow boxer*, used only here in the New Testament. What does a shadow boxer do? He literally punches the air trying to hit his own shadow. There's no real enemy to strike, so he just aimlessly swings and swings, expending all his energy but never hitting the target.

Again, Paul said, "…So fight I, not as one that beateth the air." Once more we see the Greek word *ouk*, translated here as the word "not," and it is *an emphatic form of the word no*. The word "beateth" is the Greek word *dero*, which pictures *the grueling and barbaric practice of beating someone*. And the word "air" in Greek describes *the lower, denser regions of the earth's atmosphere* or *an empty space*. Thus, Paul emphatically and categorically said, "I am not like a shadow boxer who swings aimlessly at shadows and things that don't exist. I know exactly what I'm aiming for and running to."

Learn To Exercise Control Over Your Mouth and Body

In First Corinthians 9:27, Paul wraps up his illustration by saying, "But I keep under my body, and bring it into subjection: lest that by any means, when I have preached to others, I myself should be a castaway."

As we unpack the meaning of this verse, let's begin with the phrase "I keep under." It is the Greek word *hupopiadzo*, and it means *to severely strike the lower part of the face below the eyes*. In other words, it means *to beat where the mouth is located*. Basically, Paul is saying, "If I don't get a grip on my lip, I will say things that talk me right out of my race." One expositor has translated this phrase to say, "I beat the bottom half of my face black and blue and bring it under subjection; I don't let my mouth run me. I take control of it."

Next, Paul said, "…I bring it into subjection…," which is a translation of the Greek word *doulagogeo*, which means *to lead about as a slave; to treat as a slave; to subject to stern and rigid discipline*. Moreover, it means *to keep under control or mastery; to dominate*; or *to claim as one's slave*. Here Paul is declaring, "My body is not going to control me, neither is my mouth going to run my life. I'm taking charge of the lower half of my face as well as the rest of my body. My flesh will be my slave; it's going to do what I tell it to do."

Paul then concludes by saying, "…lest that by any means, when I have preached to others, I myself should be a castaway" (1 Corinthians 9:27). First notice the word "castaway," which is the Greek word *adokimos*. It describes *one that is no longer approved*. This person is *unfit* or *rejected*; *one disapproved* or *disqualified*. A person who is *discredited, dishonored, and shamed*; hence, a *castaway*. Sadly, this person was once running in a race and had a great future, but because they didn't exercise control and dominion over their mouth and body, their flesh got the upper hand and began to dominate them. They were discredited, dishonored, and disqualified and became a *castaway*.

There is one more phrase you need to understand the meaning of, and it is "should become." It is a form of the Greek word *ginomai*, and in this case, it depicts *something that develops progressively and then suddenly overcomes one and takes him off-guard*. This is the picture of a person who made excuses for his words and actions little by little, not realizing that his flesh was slowly but surely getting stronger and stronger until one day it overpowered him and knocked him out of the race. That is how believers often get knocked out of their race.

Paul said, "I'm not going to have that happen to me. I'm bringing my mouth and body into subjection to God; I'm forcing my flesh to be my slave and obey me. After all the preaching I've done, I'm not going to be disqualified from the reward I've been waiting for all this time." Friend, this is the type of mindset you have to cultivate in order to finish your race. If you will deal with "you" — mastering your flesh and living temperate in all things — you will make it all the way to the end of your race and receive the prize!

STUDY QUESTIONS

> Study to shew thyself approved unto God, a workman that needeth not to be ashamed, rightly dividing the word of truth.
> — 2 Timothy 2:15

Of all the things that can get us into trouble, nothing can make it happen faster than our own mouth. The Bible has much to say about the power of your words. Take time to carefully reflect on these passages — identifying what God is saying in each one and what He is speaking to you personally.

1. Proverbs 18:20,21
2. James 3:2-10
3. Psalm 141:3 and Proverbs 13:3; 21:23
4. James 1:26 and Proverbs 10:19; 17:27,28
5. Psalm 34:11-14 and 1 Peter 3:8-12

PRACTICAL APPLICATION

But be ye doers of the word, and not hearers only,
deceiving your own selves.
— James 1:22

1. As you come to the end of this teaching, what would you say is your greatest takeaway from all that you have learned? What do you really want to remember — and share with others?

2. Take time to slowly read this passage in Hebrews 12:1 (*AMPC*), which also talks about the race God has called you to run:

   "Therefore then, since we are surrounded by so great a cloud of witnesses [who have borne testimony to the Truth], let us strip off and throw aside every encumbrance (unnecessary weight) and that sin which so readily (deftly and cleverly) clings to and entangles us, and let us run with patient endurance and steady and active persistence the appointed course of the race that is set before us."

3. There are two things noted in this verse that keep us from running our race: unnecessary weights and sin that entangles us. Pause and pray: *Holy Spirit, please show me any unnecessary thing I'm involved in that's weighing me down or sin that keeps tripping me up that I need to strip off and throw aside. Give me the strength to break free and stay free of these things. In Jesus' name. Amen.*

4. Do you want to run your race and make it all the way to the end? Then take a few moments to pray this prayer from your heart:

Father, Thank You for choosing me to be Your creative masterpiece. Thank You for revealing to me the powerful truths in this lesson — that I am not an accident or a mistake. You made me on purpose, for a purpose. I believe You have a specific plan for my life, and I ask You to begin revealing it to me so I can jump in the race and steadily run toward the finish line. Help me, Father, to exercise control over my mouth and my body; show me how to master my flesh and make it my slave. Empower me to make it all the way to the end of my race where I will see You face-to-face and receive the eternal rewards You have waiting. In Jesus' name. Amen.

Notes

_____

_____

_____

_____

_____

_____

_____

_____

_____

_____

_____

_____

_____

_____

_____

_____

_____

_____

_____

_____

_____

_____

_____

_____

_____

_____

_____

Notes